THE RESTLESS DECADE

Goodbye Berlin. 1933.

The Restless Decade

JOHN GUTMANN'S PHOTOGRAPHS OF THE THIRTIES

ESSAY BY MAX KOZLOFF

EDITED BY LEW THOMAS

HARRY N. ABRAMS, INC., PUBLISHERS

Project Director: Robert Morton
Designer: Dirk Luykx

Editorial work for this book was partially funded by a grant
from the National Endowment for the Arts awarded to NFS Press,
San Francisco, and San Francisco Camerawork.

Library of Congress Cataloging-in-Publication Data
Gutmann, John.
   The restless decade.
   1. United States—Social life and customs—1918–1945—
Pictorial works. 2. United States—Social conditions—
1933–1945—Pictorial works. 3. United States—Descrip-
tion and travel—1920–1940—Views. 4. Photography,
Artistic. I. Kozloff, Max. II. Thomas, Lew. III. Title.
E806.G96 1984   779′.9973917   83–15522
ISBN 0-8109-2695-4 (pbk.)

PREFACE

By Lew Thomas

The impetus for this book can be traced back to 1976 when John Gutmann gave me permission to publish a group of his photographs in the publication *Photography and Language.* In it, the photograph *"Yes, Columbus Did Discover America!"* and other images by Gutmann were accorded a privileged position as a sectional frontispiece preceding the title page. The evidence of his photographs lent the book an historical aura even though Gutmann's work at that time had had limited exposure—the major exception being a retrospective exhibition organized by John Humphrey for the San Francisco Museum of Modern Art in the same year.

Without intending to justify a relationship between the first book and the exhibition, the *Columbus* photograph (reproduced on page 45) and the installation of the exhibit nevertheless provide instructive codes for the structuring of material in this volume, the first major published collection of Gutmann's work.

The image *"Yes, Columbus Did Discover America!"* attests to the unique attitude of the photographer and his commitment to subject matter: a European explorer rediscovering America photographically! For Gutmann, subject matter determines not only the angle of perspective for recording his images of America, but also operates as a method for ordering his archives. Subjects are separated into distinct categories for purposes of organization and the cross-referencing of social and aesthetic content. It is a method Gutmann continually employs in the design of his exhibitions. The categories of this book are based on this methodology:

Automobile Culture in the USA	*pages 17–46*
Documents of the Street	*47–70*
Graffiti: Marks and Messages	*71–87*
The People	*88–106*
The Depression	*107–118*
The Human Spectacle	*119–160*

The *Columbus* photograph, however, is a perfect example of an image in which can be distilled a combination of themes that overlap categorical assignment. Though the photograph refers thematically to the omnipresent automobile—a facet of life associated with the development of American culture—it is extendable to other sections in the book where signs and written messages function simultaneously as picture and caption. Or, it may be viewed as a "Document of the Street" whose vantage point and descriptive power encourage a narrative reading. Far from undermining the coherency of the book's structure, the density of visual information and complexity of focus prevalent in many of Gutmann's photographs serve to create a system of resonance between the images and their designated categories.

Another code taken from the photographer's practice that might be considered redundant with the structure of the book is the positioning of pairs of photographs that reveal Gutmann's dual vision, his ability to see subject matter from both expressive and analytic points of view. Two pictures made of an elevator garage in Chicago (pages 20 and 21) demonstrate this approach. One picture is a classical, balanced composition; surrounded by buildings, the elevator is shown as an integral part of the urban landscape. The other, expressionistic in its diagonal perspective, depicts the elevator garage slanting backwards in the frame, an unbalanced tower of industrial architecture. Some subjects, particularly those which had an overtly surreal sense about them, were rendered with an instinct for dynamic juxtaposition and gesture. Count Basie and his High Hatters were pictured in a two-part composition (pages 136 and 137) with Basie at the rear and the High Hatters seen from worm's-eye perspective, with feet stomping and hands clapping, close to the lens. A less dramatic example of this tendency can be seen in the photographs of archery classes separated in time by three years where the angle of perspective is nearly identical, emphatically underscoring a practice that was also employed in portraiture by using two persons in the same picture.

All the signifying codes that form the structure of this book have been scrupulously selected from the practices of the photographer and the content of his pictures. Even the title of Max Kozloff's essay, "The Extravagant Depression," is in turn derived from a statement written by John Gutmann in 1979:

> Titles or captions are important to me. I try to either state a fact of reality, give information to the curious viewer or direct attention to what the picture means to me. As a rule I do not like to explain my photographs. I want my pictures to be read and explored. I believe a good picture is open to many individual (subjective) associations. I am usually pleased when a viewer finds interpretations that I myself had not been aware of. I believe that some of my best images have this ambiguity which is an essence of life. In this sense I am not interested in trying desparately to make Art but I am interested in relating to the marvelous extravagance of Life.

THE EXTRAVAGANT DEPRESSION

by Max Kozloff

Memory, according to my dictionary, is "the mental capacity or faculty of retaining and reviving impressions, or of recalling or recognizing previous experiences." To aid memory, an aggregate of photographs can hold up to view images not only of separate people, now gone, but of whole cultural periods. Receding into history, a culture—the sum of the arrangements by which a society manifests itself—leaves behind artifacts such as words, objects, and images that survive in a progressively alienated and disorderly state. What lives on in the human memory of cultures is a composite of ideas that such remnants have generated. There have been very few studies of the ways photographs enter into that composite and prejudice memory with stereotypes of their own.

Let's consider, for example, two eras, Weimar Germany and Depression America. If all evidence of them had vanished except images reiterated by photo-historians, what notions would we have of those periods?

About Germany, it would have to be said that the environment there was almost entirely urban and industrial, that the light which shined then, instead of providing a luminous atmosphere, marked off zones of great contrast and edged shapes of great precision. In this clean cityscape of pronounced junctures and seams, objects, large or small, were disposed as if, in all their existence, they had no other purpose than to form up in dynamic and serrated ranks. Though obviously inanimate in themselves, the view that sets them forth dizzies the senses.

Weimar Germany would seem to have been possessed by a desolate exhilaration. Its larger structures, its bridges, towers, smokestacks, and smelters, its assembly lines and thoroughfares, constantly suggest human use but hardly anywhere does one see a community that engages with them. There is no history behind these unweathered surfaces. When passersby occasionally appear, they exhibit only their marvelous talent for being ephemeral markers of geometrical space. Quick in their entrances and exits, unaffected in their passage by the services and stores that surround them, they have gotten crisply to their assigned places, as if guided by cue marks on the pavement. Everywhere there is offered a spectacle which resembles a theater-in-the-round, in which actors and audience can exchange roles, that is, can see and be seen from multiple perspectives.

How charged must have been the sense of living in such cities, energized by the ricochet of lines and forces, tipped sightings and plunging views! The eye traverses these urban places without reference to human scale and its habit of ordering the relative weights and proportions of things in the environment. What would account for this cantilevered view if not the most intense curiosity about how the parts of the modern city, and then the parts of its parts, are put together? A mass has no significance except to meet another, and the photograph has evidently no purpose but to emphasize the acute juncture of forms. As evidence of contemporary perception, the Weimar photograph has a great condensing power, functional, punchy, and schematic as a poster.

Even when they came close to their fellow human beings and made portraits, photographers of the period tended to exclude everything but the physiognomy, or rather, the mask. People are stared at in a dispassionate way, and though they themselves hardly conceal the imprint or the effect of their past life experiences, it's as if only the present moment counts for them, the one in which they are staring back. Over and over, they appear to be gripped by a phenomenal patience into which they settle, to allow their faces to be offered up as more or less interesting topographies of the flesh.

One photographer spends a lifetime collecting portraits of hundreds of his fellow citizens, from all professions, in order to show how they make up a society. The momentum of the portrait types alludes to the national whole. Another photographer approaches the face at exceptionally close quarters, a kind of charged proximity known to doctors and lovers, but nothing intimate is disclosed. None of these faces starts up at the violation of their personal territory. A gallery of German people from the twenties and thirties, genetically quite variable but racially only Caucasian, spreads out before our eyes. Whatever the actual social, economic, or psychological circumstances, they remain implicit or are absorbed into the expressiveness with which roles are performed.

As revealed in photographs, Depression America, by contrast to upbeat Weimar, is a fallen culture. Images of this period—no less immediate, graphic, and mobile—speak of blasted hopes, wrecked lives, and social uprootedness. Every face reflects harsh and depriving circumstances—their physical cost. When the camera visits such faces in the home, or in the fields and on the roads, the scene only confirms the calamitous lack of possibilities, a desiccated and stunted environment. Even as it makes a rare appearance, a heroic emblem of twentieth-century industry such as a steel mill is preceded by a graveyard. Instead of buoyantly levitated up high, the eye is oriented by the ground, by floors and corners, as if weighted by the force of gravity.

Quite often, although people are caught out in the open, en route, along grand horizontals, they've come to a halt. Their antique flivvers or pickups, overloaded with their pitiful, rickety household goods, have broken down or run out of gas. People frequently sag in the heat (which reminds you how thermally neutral was Weimar photography). With so many of these pictures, the space through which figures walk or work is discouraging in its spread. The way in which the images suggest the plain hardness of getting anywhere is not so evident, but the fact of it is pretty clear. So, too, are the gnarledness of hands, the grudging harvests, and the rawness of unpainted wood. On balance, it's understood that the Depression in America took place only in the country and occasionally its small towns, all of which, as it happens, were located in the South and West.

This documentation of national adversity as regional experience weighs heavily on the remembering mind. By focusing on the reluctance of the nourishing land, it implies that the failures at work in this culture had natural rather than social or political causes. To be sure, there are images of authority, such as county sheriffs, and glimpses of social oppression on the faces of blacks. But mainly these out-of-work farmers, migrants, and sharecroppers are shown as splendidly natural in themselves, afflicted but resilient and stalwart. Their clothes, body language, facial expressions, and modest domestic articles are studied affectionately and respectfully. It is as if catastrophe had brought out what was most dignified in their carriage and admirable in their character. These virtues seem always to have been linked with their atavistic (to city-dwellers) way of life. Not for them the blandishments of new-car riding or speedy trains, which ironically smile down on them from occasional signs. Theirs is a world of clapboard country churches and roadside watermelon markets advertising foods at heartbreakingly low prices. Elsewhere, the industrial twentieth century may be racing ahead, into a future of steam, iron, and flight, but compared to this flinty reality, so rooted in the goodness of a rural American past, it is a phantasm only, an irrelevant and rather specious promise.

Epochal illustration in the history of photography is one of the more beguiling areas into which images have been classified. It establishes a canon of normal perceptions and typical subjects which accrete only to reinforce each other. If a picture is allowed into the corpus of Weimar photography, or seems to belong there, it's because of its analytic attitudes, its space, accented as if by points in a network, its detached emphasis on phenomena rather than history.[1] Despite its thrusting diagonals, it would have to exhibit a static conception of time, an ideal, indissoluble presentness, self-contained as is all Utopian imagery.

To be a representative Depression photo, the work must warmly examine the local particulars of a collective tragedy. It's then further required to dwell on the merits of the past as compared with a problematic future, and to insist on the *spiritual* riches of a materially impoverished society. Psychologically, the viewer of the Weimar photograph is handed a considerable power, as if to control all the vectors of the setting. The Depression picture, however, radiates the hope that power, or more accurately, well-being, ought to be shared more equitably between subject and viewer than is presently the case.[2] Any photographer of those times who did not understand that Weimar meant technological modern (even landscapes looked streamlined) and that the Depression was folksy rural would be considered marginal. He or she would stand little chance of being incorporated into the core—that core which extends down into our cultural memory and fixes there a capsule consciousness of the past.

Suppose an epochal photographer, born in Germany and nurtured by Weimar, escaped with an open state of mind from the Third Reich, in time to join the American Depression. The mutant possibilities of such a career would be hard to conceive, were it not for the revelation of John Gutmann's photographs.[3]

It was his good fortune to have gotten under way as an artist in his homeland but to have come of age, as a photographer, in his adopted country. What he carried with him and what he learned were fused vitally into an unexpected pictorial enterprise. In acting as an instinctual broker between the visual value systems of the milieu he left and the one he entered, between two time and space frames, therefore, Gutmann mingled the look of them.

If that happened to his advantage, it was also, of course, his liability. From the viewpoint of period stereotypes in photography, he kept on noticing the wrong things and working in the wrong style—calmly, devotedly, at the highest level. His work was not just put to the side; it never made the historical list. Fifty years after his arrival in America, at a moment intensely curious about the way photographs actually affect memory, John Gutmann still enters his darkroom and brings forth from it, as if they were dividends from light-hearted and long-forgotten deposits, many images he rarely printed and that were never published.

Born in Breslau in 1905, and raised there, Gutmann was one of those many sons of well-off Jewish parents who became intellectuals or went into the arts. He looks back upon his artistic training, as a master-student in painting under Otto Müller, one of the original members of Die Brücke, with a fondness for its strict discipline. (A weekly average of twenty hours life-drawing for four years trained his eyes "forever" in the appearances of the figure.) In 1933, at age 28, with an evidently promising future as a painter and art professor, Gutmann saw all of his prospects terminated by the Hitler government, when it proscribed him from any further public career.

Not wanting to stay where he was not wanted, Gutmann planned his departure. He bought a Rolleiflex, read the instruction manual, shot three rolls, had them store-developed and contact printed, and fobbed himself off as a globe-trotting photojournalist at the Berlin agency Presse-Photo, which promptly contracted him for—as he deliriously failed to notice—*exclusive* world rights to his work. Soon after, he left Germany, light of load but heavy with camera: destination, United States. This escape artist had not wanted to steal a job from those suffering chronic unemployment and reckoned that being a reporter from a European news agency was an equitable solution. "Don't stay in Europe," a friend said. "The only country you want to go to is the U.S. The only state is California. The only city, San Francisco."

Disembarking from their freighter, Gutmann and his fellow passengers looked upon a multi-racial group of shrieking, laughing, and gesticulating people. To this day, he remembers vividly how they all belonged happily together yet looked so different. After ten minutes of explanation, though amazed and delighted, he still did not know what it meant that they were shooting craps. This bird's-eye view of Orientals, blacks, whites, Indians, and Mexicans in real community became his most enduring memory of Americans.

Just about everyone in John Gutmann's photographs exhales and inhales easily; the era of stressed performance is over. Far from being beaten down by the sun, people take it in naturally, and assume that it will warm them. With the steepest diagonals in the West, San Francisco was designed to make any Weimar shutterbug trigger-happy. Yet Gutmann also discovered the first drive-in movies and restaurants (in southern California, 1935), and made their portraits. Glittering drum majorettes teased his camera. Diving into or emerging from Olympic-sized pools, swimmers with rivulets of water over their skin excited his attention. A giant historical pageant, replete with cowboys, Indians, and conquistadors, drew his bead. Nor would his world have been complete without Count Basie, the circus aerialists, the Winged Pegasus, the car parks and golf links, the beauty contests, the tattoo parlors and graffiti artists, the movie marquees, and the early girlie magazines which we know existed in the thirties but are startled to see there.

What is it that radiates from these photographs and makes us blink, giving us the feeling that we have walked those streets, have known their rhythms intimately, but had never viewed them? The Farm Security Administration (FSA) photographs of this same period are salted away yet fabled in history. They are like a sad dream, affecting yet remote. Weimar photography had no nominal truck with specific historic incident. With their compounded visual interest, though, Gutmann's images mature out of it, and sparkle with a bright pathos. The vantage assumed in many of them is that of the normal pedestrian, but the eye is that of an astonished foreigner. For him, average and nondescript scenes and fixtures, unlikely to be noticed by natives, had a riveting excitement, even a shock value. He could not anticipate what sorts of things would make pictures in this new city, but he had a readiness to see, unheard of among anyone who lived there. This was not the promiscuous enthusiasm of the greenhorn who blunders into what is taken to be a garden of delights. Young people startled by his images today are as much foreigners to his scenes in time as he was in space. In his work the familiar and unfamiliar oscillate in a way that is as much disquieting as it is pleasurable.

Before arrival, his few ideas of America had been fed by sources like Dreiser, jazz, and Chaplin. Upon settling in, he instantly engaged with what would be a life-long theme, the icons of American popular culture, which orient all behavior and affect all moods. The era conjured up by this popular culture is novel to our eyes because it is implausibly *staid* as it is also raunchy. More innocent and yet more bereaved than our own era, it nevertheless reaches out insinuatingly to us through that same hot continuum of the media that bonds us now in our diversity.

There is, then, a structural similarity, which John Gutmann could not have previsioned, between the way he looked at America and the way we examine it in the present. Many photographers who came after him have exploited this ubiquity of the media, and have educated us with it. In Gutmann's work they should have to acknowledge a major and unknown predecessor. We're more at home, though, with his manner of seeing than with the content of his vision. As he surfaces it, the decade of the American thirties had more surprising circumstantial life—more snap, gaiety, contradiction, and bite—than was ever thought stored away in still photographs.

The FSA photographers treated of vernacular, which is a very different thing from popular culture. Mainly we think of vernacular as utterly native or indigenous. It's how people fix up their immediate territories when they're at their most familial, with what they can afford or what's been handed down . . . or sometimes, with what little is left to them. The Okie homesteader's truck is, above all, a packet of vernacular articles. Nothing underlines better the rhetorical power of the FSA photographers—Dorothea Lange, say, or Ben Shahn—than the degree to which they make you empathize with vernacular objects, expressive and personal possessions in an economy of great scarcity.

An artifact of popular culture, on the other hand, cannot presume to such authenticity or preciousness. It qualifies as popular by its participation in a national mindscape, shaped and standardized by a consumer economy. Popular forms have greater range—since they cut across classes—but in Gutmann's hands, just as much idiosyncrasy as vernacular ones. It makes little difference who owns them or how long they last because they function as ephemeral diffusers of social myths, partly imposed upon, but mostly commanded by, the industrial order which transmits the general modes of egalitarian consciousness. John Gutmann showed extraordinary sensitivity to popular culture—which he describes and analyzes rather than endorses—possibly because he saw in it a much more amiable, exotic, and malleable counterpart of what would have been repugnantly familiar to him in Germany under the name propaganda.[4]

As an emblem of a society where the class structure is open and fluid, rather than rigidly bound and hierarchically ordered, the key motif in Gutmann's photography is the automobile. Photographers may have celebrated mass production in Weimar but gave no clue as to how it was used or how it changed people's experience. In California, the car acted as a sign of profligate but necessary mobility, through all the walks of life as well as space. Students went to the Galileo High School in roadsters and coupes. Of a culture whose young naturally assume such privileges, how could one say it was in the doldrums? When he saw people travel to unemployment lines in cars, Gutmann ceased taking seriously any national cries of despair or mutterings about revolution.

In Germany, giving high status to the few who could buy and maintain them, sedans were still badges of affluence. At Chicago, though, he spotted a ten-story, free-standing elevator that parked them by the score—clearly a great visual wonder and something of a folly. It would have occurred only to a foreigner that America was blessed in not having to worry about squandering its metals. Weimar had articulated the *progressive*, a state of being which had not yet gotten its circulation and which was expressed through an expectant neatness of things, in the end absurdly chaste. But here, in America, was progress itself, in the now, and it turned out *not* to be Modern in the orderly sense at all, but bumptiously prolific, ingenious, and convenient. Motorists, for example, could get snacks served on trays clamped to their open car windows. And Mobilgas customers were advised to use a credit card in driving to the New York World's Fair (1939).

Looking at John Gutmann's cars, you can thumb a ride through the American thirties. There are not too many of these vehicles, at first, nor are there traffic jams, but they make up for their scanty number by being great characters. To be sure, they all start off having the same die-stamped, square-jawed configuration, and they wear black, like deacons or undertakers. Under the California sun, which Gutmann etches brilliantly, this sobriety has a faintly comical air— like that of stiff Victorians at a loss in lotus-land. Soon enough, though, he peeks in car windows, sees cheesecake decals, or looks close at the chrome-winged fripperies of hood ornaments. A Wyoming license plate with rodeo silhouette or a dashboard with a picture of a prancing deer will not yield to car culture the myth of a wilder West. In 1934, someone out there draped a saddle over the hood of a two-seater. By 1936, when Gutmann got to Harlem, on a great continental bus odyssey, he shows a Cord, with its fabulous modern grille, flanked heraldically by two expensively dressed black men. The more discrepant its realities, the livelier and more comprehensive was Gutmann's photographic report.

Autos, certainly, were not just isolated social data in the cityscape; their backup and support systems—the gas stations and used-car lots, businesses that had their own typical sign codes—also fed into it. They are described in a thoroughgoing spirit, as if the photographer were filling in essential parts of a text. In the beginning of his 1971 book on Los Angeles, Reyner Banham writes: " . . . like earlier generations of English intellectuals who taught themselves Italian in order to read Dante in the original, I learned to drive in order to read Los Angeles in the original." Gutmann reveals that certain cars themselves, hand printed all over with messages, were meant to be read. One of them warns that the "Lies Are Falling Thick and Fast" and that "the International Bankers Have Taken it [America] Away From Us Saps," sentiments continued in a nearby awning with a more explicit putdown of Roosevelt as a friend of the money-changers.[5] This turns out to be a bit of private electioneering on behalf of retirement warranties, made all the more irate and hectoring by the starkness of the white lettering on the black car paint.

Just as interesting, though, are the misspellings, the crackerjack diction, and the plain-folks tone. Elsewhere, prowling the streets, Gutmann picked up this same phenomenon in painted posters and billboards. "Taste Be 4 U Buy," "Jeepers Creepers!": the colloquial voice may reflect something of the influx of country people into the cities, but it is also, so to speak, the vernacular aspiring to be popular.

Or rather, it's a kind of John-Doe street literature, knowingly cartooned in order to oppose itself to ideologies spread by newspapers and government. By contrast, public typography, during the early thirties, was as serifed as the roofs, cowlings, and fenders of Fords. This slangier script had far less rectitude, and adds vividly to Gutmann's inventory of the decade's argot. He had been prepared for skyscrapers, but not for the American commonplace, neither its nerve nor its ironies and freedoms. Demotic messages of this sort do appear in Walker Evans, and also in Berenice Abbott, whose important photography was not necessarily centered by the Depression. For Abbott, in New York, storefront advertising speaks of the display forms of ethnic migration and mom/pop enterprise, reminiscent of the Europe from which she had lately returned. Gutmann, however, was more absorbed by all sorts of gripes, folk humor, eroticism, crankiness, and the voices of protest. In short, the sorts of messages that were repressed in Germany.

In his outlook, the have-nots, the out-of-work, and the dispossessed resort to written statements, and the air resounds with their pleas and their causes. Framing these underground utterances seems to have been Gutmann's way of informing himself and of telling his viewers what was going on beneath the surfaces of middle-class society. There is a lot of language in his pictures, and people reading it, as if to encourage us to do the same. "Looky," or "We Want the 40 Hour Week," "Nazi Agents in San Francisco," "Boycott Japanese Buy American" (this last a complaint by the Chinese community against the Japanese invasion of China, though it sounds very much like a latter-day pitch by American automobile manufacturers!). Thirties culture is abuzz with alarms and discontent. This is not yet the specific trauma of the Depression, but a tally of flawed, grating, and malignant conditions, even some current events, all very particular in themselves, but reflective of a more diffused and polyglot stress.

Though it has its smiling faces, Gutmann's work was never intended to show that things were going well, or that they would necessarily turn out badly. Its author has written, simply, that he was "interested in relating to the *marvelous extravagance of life*" (italics added). Professionally speaking, John Gutmann was a journalist; emotionally, a celebrant; intellectually, a historian. The "marvelous extravagance of life" was rooted in an American world he never made, but with which he was thoroughly engaged. The fact that it was restive and tendentious (like most modern periods, but with a cadence of its own) only made it the more intense in its extravagance.

In order to do justice to that intensity, Gutmann considered its furthest regressions, its most intimate and humble signs. Instead of portraying the more obvious human casualties on the street, he framed some of their graffiti. Here are individual fantasies of power, expressions of hate and revenge, apologies, and homilies, far removed from the more social utterances of politics and business. They belong to an underclass of communications, assertive yet abbreviated. Photography, here, acts as an equivalent of oral history—retrieving lost scraps of ordinary lives—though necessarily cryptically and evocatively.[6] No one can tell for which audience, if any, the graffiti were scribbled, nor who originated them. Even when a message is addressed to people with such wonderfully thirties names as "Sophie" and "Mae," of whom a graffito complains that they missed their appointment, we do not know where or when. It could have been written a year or a day before Gutmann photographed it. Complete, yet leaving a great deal unspoken, it deposits no further track into memory than itself. Still, while anonymous, tentative, and often superimposed disrespectfully upon each other, the graffiti have a self-interestedness and loopy freedom, combining words and drawing, that border on the artistic. Gutmann tells us as much when he titles a shot of a Chinese kid chalking a figure of an American Indian on a street, while dark cars pass by, *The Artist Lives Dangerously* (page 73).

In photographic terms, the images of the graffiti, though they include poignant material, are copies that do not presume any visual initiatives of their own. They are remarkable, on the contrary, for their quality of attention, which has a moral value. They simply attend to archaic human markings, of which no one was aware enough even to judge them unworthy of attention. It was not despite his wide scope, but as a virtue of it, that Gutmann could conceive of operating at this modest level. Though he enthusiastically welcomes variable responses to his work, he denies that it was artistically motivated. It was rather with the instincts "of a child," as he said, made ecstatic by a "new toy" that he felt released from "formalistic art concepts."

Childlike instinct, just the same, does not account for the adult perceptions and the worldly coverage of his photography. His nominal Depression pictures were sent back, on contract, for European consumption, where they were placed by Presse-Photo, and eventually other agencies, in journals such as *Der Welt Spiegel, Die Woche,* and *Berliner Illustrierte Zeitung.* (Some of his pictures were used by Nazi organs, a fact over which he had no control.) By 1936, breaking with Presse-Photo, he was able to sign with Pix, Inc., N.Y., which placed his work in *Life, Saturday Evening Post, Time.* Later, he worked directly for *Coronet,* one of the more enlightened pictorial journals of the forties.

Occasionally he would propose themes and at other times he would accept assignments. Even when photographing free-lance for the American magazines, though, he employed certain tactics required by their European counterparts, the early leaders in the field. It goes a long way toward understanding the explicitness of American scenography in Gutmann's photographs to know that foreign editors wanted him to establish his milieu. A billboard advertising Dodge cars or a poster for Coca-Cola localized his reporting. The racial mix of the large American cities was an initial and continuing source of attraction to him, especially since "that maniac" had demanded that everyone in Germany be Aryan. Unless he could declare, though, that these were *Chinese-Americans,* rather than Chinese, his exposition would not be judged clear enough for his audiences in Europe. With its strong cueing and internal captions, his work accommodated itself to its reportorial context while it also articulated his own interests.

Though very capable of satisfying journalistic rules for "human interest," picture stories, and news events, Gutmann fused the information content of his photographs with elements of observation and feeling tones that were much more personal. No one in an editorial office required his work to be as insistent, reflective, and searching as it quite often was. Not the topic or the anecdote interested him so much as the life around him, a continuous activity that revealed itself gradually through its unannounced gestures and its unpredictable voices. Because no market existed for his particular sympathies, a great quantity of Gutmann's work was inevitably private, undertaken for his own pleasure. The distinction between this intimate aspect of his photography and the evidently more commercial work is still not a clear one. It was simply a happy chance that the imagery needing to be narratively climactic financed that which he wanted to be psychologically pointed, and that the two unfolded into each other.

As examples of harrowing density and concision, perceived by a highly observant eye, compare "*Ham and Eggs,*" of 1938 (page 65), with *Guns for Sale,* 1936 (page 97). These are simultaneously street portraits, genre scenes, and symbolic statements.[7] In the first, an elderly couple stands together: she reading the radical newspaper *Ham and Eggs* (with a strident headline "Persecution Stirs Statewide Anger"); he, behind her, blind and possibly scowling. Next to them, in a watchmaker's window, are placards quoting the Gettysburg Address: "Of . . . For the People," etc., and a notice of retirement warranties. The juncture of these particular individuals and their sign environment is politically combustible without being didactic. Grimmer, but just as fortuitous, is the picture of two shabby black men, caught a second before stepping out of the frame towards us. Momentarily illuminated by sunlight latticed through the New York "El" above them, their eyes hooded by shadow under their hat brims, they have just passed a street vitrine loaded with shotguns and ammo. In these photographs, two rapid glances at very different subjects yield frames implicit with foreboding, irony, and violence. In one continuous circuit, they weld together disturbing wholes out of fractious parts. To a photographer with such synthetic powers of vision, demonstrated over and over again, the decade could not help betraying itself.

People did a lot of waiting during that period. If it was an experience that typifies our recall of the thirties, it presented a challenge to photographers because they had to make exposure time count in the act of showing how social time was being wasted. A picture cannot analyze systemic breakdown, but it can suggest how the intervals between actions begin to stretch, how loneliness, boredom, and a sense of inadequacy begin to infect the community as an enforced leisure steals over it. Ever concrete, Gutmann describes, with single figures or groups, queued up or scattered, how racism and bureaucracy contribute to this state of affairs. Even so, commerce does not cease to make its appeals, and a sign above the heads of a street crowd engaged in one of those recurring ceremonies of idleness innocently asks, "Do You Need Money?" What is happening in these scenes of displacement and listlessness, so energetically observed? The answer is, nothing, itself a major event. But that very fact, the void that it represents, is productive of symbolism.

It was possible at any moment in this world of fifty years ago to turn a corner and be taken aback. For the view that opens up, as John Gutmann's Depression wears on, is sundered, as if it is running on two timetables simultaneously. So many of the average functions of the city, its transport, media, and communications, as well as its established architecture, strike one suddenly as of the bright-eyed past, or at least as unrelated to the present aimless and unstable reality of people on the streets. In the country, one would certainly have perceived that conditions were terribly amiss, but not that the times were seriously out of joint. Evidence of this schism was constantly hatching in role reversals, in unexplained absences or new presences, minor incongruities, untoward incidents and ominous potentials. Confronted with these circumstances, and having to make sense of them, *Gutmann was one of the first photographers to have discovered that the present could be clocked and then defined by the increment of its disjunctions.*

He did not contrive any of these phenomena, but it looks as if he had a specially attuned radar for them. Whatever else may be said of photography, it is an abrupt medium. It does not so much supply as beg or gratuitously force connections between the appearances it randomly frames. Increasingly, one sees that it is their miniature jolts that unify Gutmann's portrait of the thirties. The Mardi Gras in New Orleans (had anyone seriously photographed it before?) is already a study in social upset and tolerated license, in which a whole population is temporarily permitted to act out what it is not. Instead of being socially disenfranchised and deferential, as whites required them to be, blacks took over the street in a riotous carnival spirit. Just as contrary, it happened, one day, that the San Francisco wharves were deserted, except for squads of National Guards—prickly sentinels of space—who had moved in, with their tanks and weapons.

Gutmann's views of the San Francisco General Strike of 1934, sparked by a longshoremen's walk-out (led by Harry Bridges) that precipitated a city-wide shutdown, combine desolation and menace in a very European way. In his personal history there were memories that allowed him to visualize an artillery parade on Market Street as a decidedly more glowering and weighty affair than everyday Americans would have imagined it. Figures are shuffled into territories and hang around where they have no ordinary business; or they are aligned in alienating rhythms. Masked welders, rigidly formed up for an inspection—or so it seems—are called *Avant-Guard* (page 128). Even when he looked up, in the sky, Gutmann saw three fighter planes he knew enough to title *Omen* (page 130). Radar is a system called upon to detect intrusions in a field. For Gutmann, lines of sight gradually ceased being avenues of expected incident and were transformed into open zones, imminently transgressed. This, too, was a democratic possibility, but as much a befuddling as it was a hopeful one.

A *Navy Daddy* (page 94) with baby on a leash: what could be more trivially endowed with "human interest"? Yet a powerful, striding, dark-garbed, and rather awesome woman disrupts it and turns it into something less benign. As for the *Stock Broker Pushing Baby Carriage on Upper Broadway* (page 94), its combination of funereal pram and prim, bowler-hatted gent being domestic is ineffably ridiculous. Episodes of this sort strike one as anomalous because they disappoint or upset social stereotypes of the period. They can also imply new realities, simmering underneath, as if the community is caught in the act of transforming itself, the process coming alive in manners that had not been glimpsed before.

In the work of Henri Cartier-Bresson, André Kertész, Helen Levitt, and now John Gutmann, during the thirties, a gimlet eye traces the spectacle of urban life, finding it less and less cohesive and rational the more it is examined. With the others, the insight emerges as a freer reflex of their artistic sensibility; with Gutmann, it is tied to his involvement with his culture as an historical phenomenon. We're far from the prodigious Surrealism of the fifties and later, when popular culture became a burlesque that altered the street into an almost nonstop series of incongruities. In the thirties, we are nevertheless at the onset of this development—materially, as it begins to take hold of the setting itself, and artistically, as photographers learn how to visualize it.

Events or appearances that would start out with one kind of everyday meaning begin to turn or curdle and imply a very different sort of significance. Sometimes the occasion pivots on a matter of incidental contrast, as in Gutmann's picture of two Texas ladies, one in a Tom Mix cowboy outfit, the other in dowdy civilians. An extract from the ordinary pluralism of American dress, the photograph, just the same, throws behavioral codes into some doubt. More extreme are his photos of women in amorous dalliance or in wanton Lesbian love. Of two or more terms in the pictorial scenario, one of them stands out as being "wrong" in combination, or misplaced . . . in the context of accepted morality. But it is not just that his subjects violate standard prohibitions, consciously or not; the photographer does, too, as in the course of his work an occupational curiosity turns into a personal voyeurism.

A man startled by the "extravagance" of life does not deny that his responses to it can be sexed, amused, or mystified. While highly descriptive, the materials at his disposal were lightly determined. He saw to it that meanings could be *invented*, through angle, lighting, caption, an array of tactics coordinated with his appetites, and as he did so he devised his own fantasies about what he saw. His athletes are luminous objects of desire or incarnations of grace—as are some of his more baroque majorettes. *The Orator* (page 90) and *Cynics, Hollywood* (page 91) (the latter of newly arriving Europeans whom Gutmann felt were especially patronizing), on the other hand, are worm's-eye portrait views.

Likewise, there was no expressive necessity for the bandage on the cheek of the young Indian musician, or the fly on the forehead of Arnold Schoenberg. But these two "marks" complicate the mortal dignity of such faces. For that matter, so, too, does the bandage on the shin of the young man, naked but for loincloth, shoes, and socks, who sunbathes with eyes closed in the most abandoned attitude (page 100). As if he were a choice bouquet of desert flowers, set off by a toothy Navajo blanket, he seems to exhibit himself in a locale that also includes a background conquistador, in full regalia, taking a break, some living-room furniture, and a curve of railroad track! Whatever could have been invented here had no chance of competing with what had been discovered. Or is it that discovery, at times, is so radiant that it becomes an invention?

Though it's rarely groping or feckless, Gutmann's level of acceptance—of ill-assorted, happenstantial, and sometimes self-canceling motifs—is remarkably broad. That very broadness represents a dynamic principle, for its inclusive sense of possibilities operates on and eventually twists the view of social probabilities. Gutmann belongs to that type of still photographer keenly interested in asserting new probabilities, but whose ethics prevent him from staging them—intervening in the realities he is otherwise actively proposing. It always remains important that the viewer can intuit the contrast between the banal circumstances—such as an off-stage moment behind the set of a California historical pageant in *By the Railroad Track* discussed above—and the delirium of their effect. The fact that they don't depend on the photographer for having happened keeps these images from *insisting* on a likely symbolism. Yet it also makes them more credible as vision. They arise in the work of one receptive to "the obscure fertilities of chance," a phrase of Paul Zweig's, describing an ideal of the mythic adventurer. The real meaning of such images starts up beyond the point they can or need to be explained.

Scanning normal traffic, the photographer was on the lookout for a bogey. This would seem to be the case when Gutmann rapidly framed an aged and bony lady coming toward him, her polka-dotted frock and swinging bodice pom-poms oddly festive in contrast with her obscurely veiled face. It was certainly a worthwhile visual moment. But there lurked in it a macabre presence which Gutmann names, appropriately, and also as if for the title of a thriller, *Death Stalks Fillmore* (page 99).

From the first, the activity of mind at work in this photography had its playful side. This aspect of Gutmann's portrait of the thirties is its most equivocal feature, lending his imagery, too, its specific depth. Regardless of its disorders, the epoch presented itself to him largely as a comedy of manners. If one riffles through his pictorial archive as quickly as a deck of cards, the faces of them almost dissolving into each other, it gains a critical mass and achieves a manicky quality, illustrating the decline and inconsequential fall of practically everyone. No matter how many repeated spills it takes, the society is obviously elastic enough to pick itself right up again. Misfortune was only an interval for those who expected to be given lucky or deserving chances. Gutmann's humor is reflective and intellectually reserved, rather than satiric and, therefore, disrespectful. When he enjoyed himself, it was not at the expense of individuals, but of sentimentality and ideology, that is, of guidelines to feeling and advisories on right thinking. People are stranded in their dilemmas or are sprung from them unawares—as the mood or the setting shifts around them. It is as if the day they imagine themselves to be living has little relation to the day that can be observed in the photo.

The great (and even the lesser) Depression photographs assert, above all, that people are conscious of the one miserable, long-standing trauma that is happening to them, and that every aspect of their behavior conforms to such organizing consciousness. This highly creative approach was called "documentary," and it was as such documentary records that Depression photographs have shaped our understanding of the period. Though they existed within the same social framework, Gutmann's Americans do not seem to possess a like knowledge of their condition. His subjects are by no means as sorrowful and inward as those of his colleagues (whose work he was largely unacquainted with until after the Second World War).[8] But this is not because Gutmann's characters are somehow more innocent, or exempt from material pressure. Their reality, rather, was more perplexing. Which means, too, that our privileged grasp of it is conflicted and elusive. The photographer's playfulness elides into a gentle irony.

Given this patchwork environment, the ironist has an advantage over those whose view of the period is more homogeneous. But the multiple icons of John Gutmann are also reflected through his multiple techniques. His photographic gestures can no more be pinned down to one formulaic approach than his tableaux can be said to describe only one social arena of life, or express one level of emotional response. Pictorially as well as psychologically, he perceives the decade as a theater-in-the-round.

The photographic scrimmage is always redefined by the opportunities that unfold before him, and not by an operational program. With him, the latitudes of intrusion are finely gradated and empirically determined, trade-offs, possibly, between what was photographically necessary for him and psychologically tolerable to his subjects. Long-shots and mid-shots alternate with frequent close-ups. Gutmann is just as liable to shoot things against the light as he is to have the light behind him. A salient detail may draw focus away from a central image. He has no preferences for arrested movement over blurred action, when called for. The camera may distort space at extreme angles as much as it accords to appearances an everyday vantage.

These images are as finely crafted and as seriously printed as they can be. For all the mobility of their perception, and their fluctuating stances, Gutmann's photographs are neither stylistically loose nor arbitrary. We are not dealing with a cameraman so badgered by his instincts that every photographic act turns out to be a professional emetic. It's a question, rather, of a photographer with a very strong character and also a large visual vocabulary, who does not hesitate to employ them in order to give an account of his equally large human and social themes.

Nowhere are his mastery over variable modes, and his bravura performance, so evident as in his framing. Gutmann speaks of having acquired his pictorial security in his training as a painter. When it came to exploring what his "new toy" could do, incisive framing was not a virtue, not an end in itself, but a base requirement, a way of formulating content, which he took for granted. Initially, any photographer confronts a kind of inarticulate "waste" and the visual product that is fished out of it is determined by the frame, as much a temporal as it is a spatial enclosure. Something absolutely inherent in a photograph, its historical occasion, is rounded off right away and finished with, as soon as light hits film. Instantly draining its strategic reserves, the photograph stakes the revelation of content on the realization of the frame. The two come together simultaneously, refract each other, or else fail to communicate.

In surroundings that offered him no professional community, the young refugee John Gutmann had no choice but to invent himself as a photographer. From memories of the German illustrated press and the jangle of American culture, experienced first hand, he fashioned his own peppy, pictorial amalgam. As a rule, the greater the amount of social information he wanted to transmit, the calmer and more centered was his framing. Reciprocally, the more tremulous the action that beckoned him—and he was an adept of action—the more off-plumb are his weights and the more kinetic are the interrupting edges of the picture. *Out of the Pool* (page 141) and *Portrait of Count Basie* (page 137) are stunning examples of American subjects and German framing—angular and synthetic in their energies, armpit- and calf-high in their sighting, witty and involving in their human textures.

Interspersed throughout Gutmann's record of the American thirties are moments like these, genial moments of pleasure lived at full throttle. They may have about them a distinction of jazzy rhythm or a tingle of the flesh. The decade, after all, was not so driven to resemble our dismal memory of it that such historically undifferentiated moments were at a minimum. For Gutmann, they, too, were part of "the marvelous extravagance" of life. But his sense of it was uniquely conditioned by *his* history. Existing within his own consciousness, he nevertheless knew that he was observing everyone else's world as well as his own. In his way, at his own pace (systematically, as it turned out), he pictured an historical epoch. Throughout his campaign, very similar subjects recur, though they are very differently handled. If his sampling was more encyclopedic (a fairly European trait) and more contradictory than our stereotypes are prepared for, that is no denigration of the period, nor of his judgment. His past collided with and was humanized by his present, as though the ideal and the material, as principles, had come wonderfully to terms with each other. If it's the mark of the true modern to accommodate to rapidly dislocating experiences, then here is a modernist, incarnate.

But the mnemonic power of the photograph can also rescue us from the trance into which modernism falls when it wants to forget history (unfortunately, a great deal of the time). When compared to our *photographic* recollection of the thirties, the one that has been established as a true memorial, Gutmann nevertheless kept a different set of carbons. In them, popular culture gets on very comfortably with vernacular expression, and economic malaise coexists with casual affluence. We were aware of that, of course, but we hadn't visualized it, at least in that medium which enjoys the highest prestige as the medium of record.

As more of its history is made visible to us, though, it is seen that photography is an ongoing system of corrective visions that undermine but also supplement each other. That spectacle is very instructive, for it teaches that one's knowledge of oneself as an integral being in time is livened by an enhanced perception of what is owed to memory. One sees, too, how much the present can communicate with the past, and one can calculate more finely those degrees by which "now" had been anticipated by "then." When that happens we're also not so quick, in fact we tend to postpone judgments of where we are. "If I am no longer young," wrote Jules Renard, "I should like to know at what hour of what day my youth left me." It is one of their most refreshing and vivid reassurances that the photographs of John Gutmann do not yet answer that kind of question.

Notes

1. Only in the last three years have studies been published on important exceptions to this Weimar photographic canon. They are: Friedrich Seidenstucker, *Von Weimar bis zum Ende Fotografien aus bewegter Zeit,* Harenberg, Dortmund, 1980, and Walter Ballhause, *Sozialdokumentarische Fotografie 1930–1933 Zwischen Weimar und Hitler,* Schirmer/Mosel, Munchen, 1981. Both Seidenstucker and Ballhause emerge as interesting combinations of street journalists and "concerned" photographers. The fact that such picture-makers, involved directly with the concrete living conditions of their period, have been virtually ignored up to now, reflects on the political inclinations of photo-historians. For that matter, we still have to wait for extended scholarly work on the AIZ, the Communist Arbeiter Illustrierte Zeitung, a vast archive of radical photographs of the Interregnum.

2. Naturally enough, in view of the fact that FSA photographs were funded by an agency of the Roosevelt administration, which had promised that the benefits of the nation's wealth would be equalized among all the people. The photographers could be said to have internalized this policy, or rather, campaign pledge.

3. It is true that a number of important photographers had emigrated to the United States from Germany during the thirties. They include Alfred Eisenstaedt, Martin Munckasci, and later, Horst P. Horst. These men had worked in several European countries and had established reputations as commercial photographers. None of them can be described as interested in "epochal illustration."

4. From one of his already characteristic first rolls, there appears, down a Berlin street, a prominent store sign advertising SS uniforms.

5. A well-justified accusation. In *Indispensable Enemies: The Politics of Misrule in America,* Penguin Books, 1974, p. 110, Walter Karp writes: "The legislation of the First New Deal began with the Emergency Banking Relief Act. If Congressional reformers had expected Roosevelt to strip from the discredited bankers their private control of the nation's credit, they were fatally disappointed. At public expense Roosevelt restored the bankers' power under the guise of emergency legislation. . . . Further New Deal banking legislation would permanently consolidate the big banks' control over the nation's credit, control which the majority of Americans had vainly opposed for decades."

6. Gutmann was not the only photographer to have been captivated by graffiti. Seidenstucker did some very charming pictures of them, sometimes in the process of being made—and then there were also Helen Levitt and Brassaï. Said Brassaï: "Walls attract me by their graffiti, because, in our civilization, they replace nature." The rather aboriginal, and certainly abstract character of Brassaï's graffiti perhaps bears out this idea of a replacement of nature. Could it be that the presence of script in them would have been too citified? Gutmann, by contrast, almost never intrudes a natural reference into his city scenes.

7. Speaking of the Social Security Act, Karp (ibid., p. 118) writes: "In no other welfare system in the world did the state shirk all responsibility for old-age indigency and insist that funds be taken out of the current earnings of workers." The aged poor were waiting then, and still wait, for legislation that would improve their lot. Gutmann's photo is particularly graphic in this respect. Incidentally, the historical reference of the newspaper is to Upton Sinclair's campaign slogan "Ham and Eggs and Thirty Dollars a Week. . . ." Sinclair was defeated.

8. Interestingly, Gutmann relates that at his 1947 show at the M. H. de Young Memorial Museum, titled "Face of the Orient," he was complimented briefly by an old lady whose name, as he only learned afterward, was Dorothea Lange!

Automobile Culture in the USA

"Switch to Dodge." Detroit, 1936.

Cord in Harlem. New York, 1936.

Elevator Garage with Parking Lot. Chicago, 1936.

Elevator Garage. Chicago, 1936.

Used Car Lot. San Francisco, 1939.

Used Car Row, Van Ness Avenue.
San Francisco, 1935.

Automobile Transport. Chicago, 1936.

"Cash for Your Car." San Francisco, 1939.

Elephant Tower on Treasure Island (Golden Gate International Exposition). San Francisco, 1939.

Automobiles Parked at a Beach. Oregon, 1934.

Parking in the Park.
San Francisco, 1935.

*Students' Cars Parked
at Galileo High School.*
San Francisco, 1934.

American Landscape II. Cleveland, 1936.

"Hack Stand."
New York, 1936.

American Landscape I.
Cleveland, 1936.

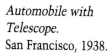

Automobile with Telescope.
San Francisco, 1938.

Piggyback: Soap Box Derby.
San Francisco, 1936.

Chinese Laundry.
San Francisco, 1934.

The New Gadget.
San Francisco, 1935.

Bicycle of a Mexican Barber. San Antonio, 1937.

The Saddle. Rodeo Salinas, California, 1934.

Reach. San Francisco, 1938.

The Dragon. San Francisco, 1938.

California License Plate. 1939.

Texas Car. 1937.

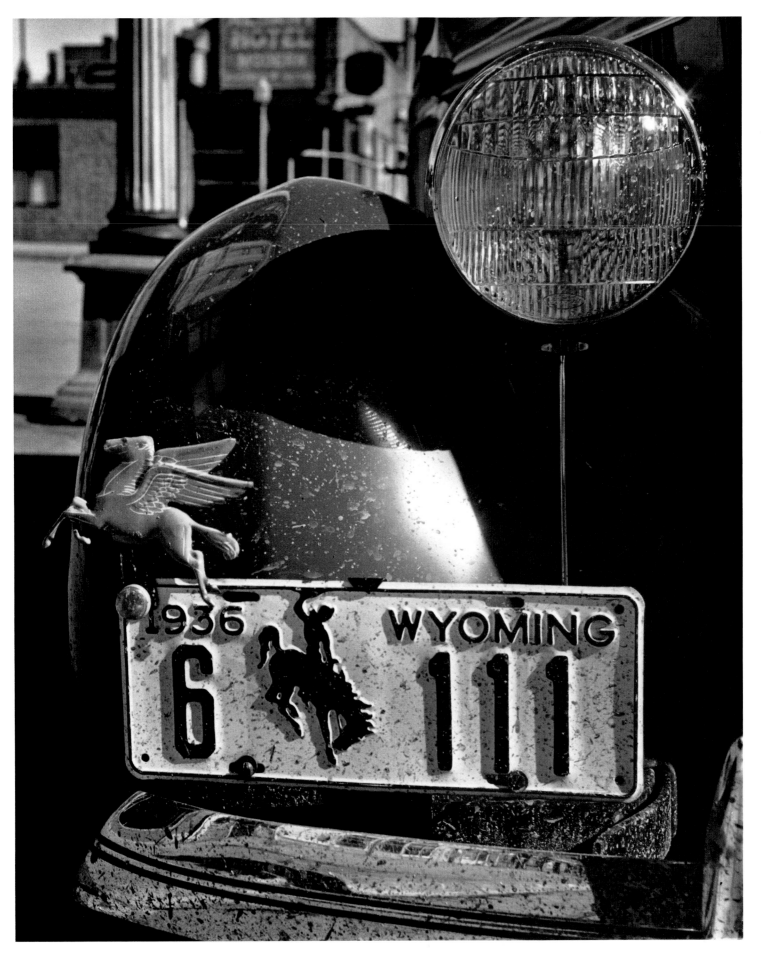

Wyoming Car. 1936.

Dashboard with Deer. California, 1938.

Mystery Bumper Sticker.
Oregon, 1939.

The Decal. 1935.

"God is Love." San Francisco, 1939.

Early Drive-In Restaurant. Hollywood, 1935.

"Eat in Car." Early Drive-In Restaurant, Hollywood, 1935.

First Drive-In Theatre. Los Angeles, 1935.

Inside the First Drive-In Theatre. Los Angeles, 1935.

Car at Election Time. San Francisco, 1938.

"Yes, Columbus Did Discover America!" San Francisco, 1938.

*San Francisco Celebrates the
Opening of the World's Fair.* 1939.

"Cut Your Speed." San Francisco, 1935.

Documents of the Street

"We Love Our Children." San Francisco, 1935.

The Trash Can Man. San Francisco, 1935.

Pop Advertising. San Francisco, 1939.

Creole Menu. New Orleans, 1937.

"Ten Cents a Meal." San Francisco, 1935.

Sign. California, 1937.

"Silk Hat Harry, The Only Colored Juggler in San Francisco." 1938.

Girlie Mags. San Francisco, 1937.

Burlesque on Broadway. San Francisco, 1934.

Checking Out the Latest Magazines.
San Francisco, 1937.

"Vanishing Gangsters."
San Francisco, 1934.

Males Inspecting Burlesque Display. San Francisco, 1934.

Chinatown Boys Looking at Military Charts. San Francisco, 1937.

Kids Reading Comics. San Francisco, 1938.

Chinese Boy Looking at Display of Warplane Models. San Francisco, 1938.

"Aviation Club." Chinatown, San Francisco, 1937.

Declaration of Protest. Chinatown, San Francisco, 1935.

Anti-Fascist Posters. San Francisco, 1938.

"We Want the 40 Hour Week." San Francisco, 1934.

Workers Studying E.R.A. Project Announcement. San Francisco, 1934.

"WPA." San Francisco, 1937.

"Ham and Eggs." San Francisco, 1938.

Employment Agency. New York, 1936.

"Barber School." Bowery, New York, 1936.

"End of the Trail."
Reno, Nevada, 1936.

*Gambling in Reno Casino
at Election Time.*
Nevada, 1936.

Black Jack in Reno at Election Time. Nevada, 1936.

Gamblers at 5:15 AM. Reno, Nevada, 1936.

Graffiti:
Marks and Messages

Street Boys with Graffiti.
San Francisco, 1938.

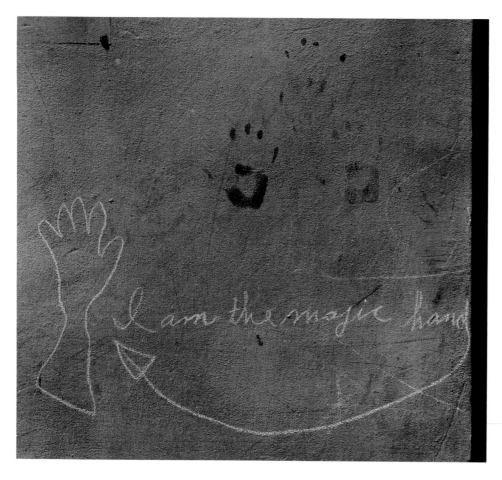

"I am the Magic Hand."
San Francisco, 1937.

The Artist Lives Dangerously. San Francisco, 1938.

The Monkey. San Francisco, 1938.

Freaky Faces Graffiti.
San Francisco, 1939.

Female Figure Graffito. San Francisco, 1938.

One-Eyed Woman Graffito. San Francisco, 1939.

Soldier Passing by Lady Graffito. San Francisco, 1939.

Man Walking by Clown and Lady Graffiti. San Francisco, 1939.

Love-Hate Graffiti. New Orleans, 1937.

Date Book. San Francisco, 1939.

"We Are Here But Where Are You?"
San Francisco, 1936.

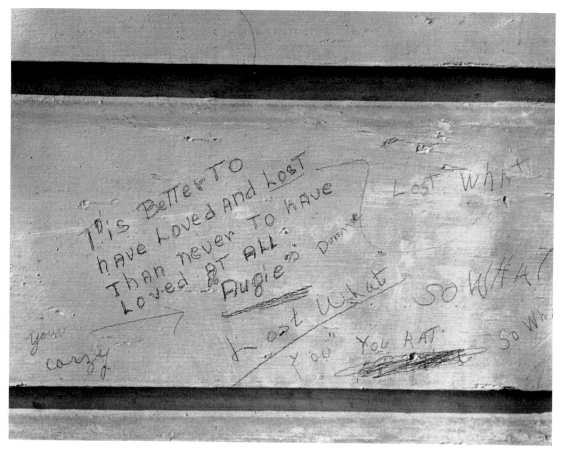

"Lost What."
San Francisco, 1938.

Apology. San Francisco, 1938.

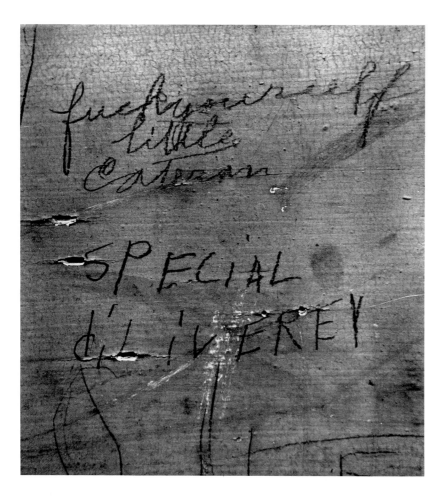

"Fuck Yourself Little Caterin." San Francisco, 1938.

"Do You Want a Screw."
San Francisco, 1939.

Against! San Francisco, 1939.

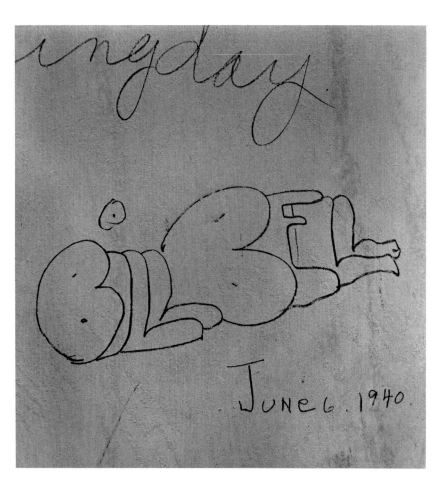

Erotic Signature. San Francisco, 1940.

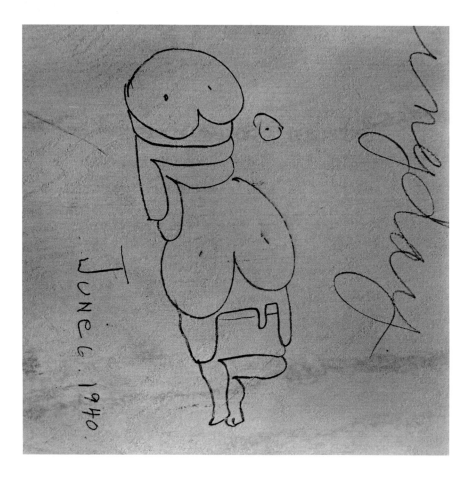

Erotic Signature. San Francisco, 1940.

Waterfront Graffiti. San Francisco, 1938.

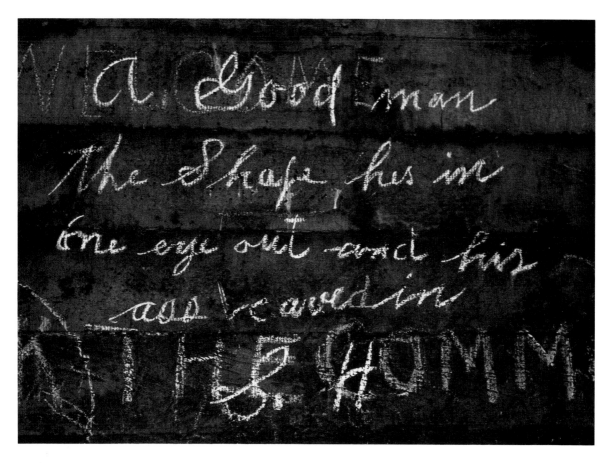

Longshoreman's Poem.
Waterfront,
San Francisco, 1938.

*Longshoreman Graffiti
with CIO Dove.*
Waterfront,
San Francisco, 1939.

"Baron Von Hoffman for President." San Francisco, 1938.

The News Photographer. San Francisco City Hall, 1935.

The People

The Orator. 1939.

Cynics, Hollywood. 1934.

In the Background: The Pimp. New Orleans, 1937.

Horse and Hand. San Francisco, 1935.

Stock Broker Pushing Baby Carriage on Upper Broadway.
New York, 1936.

Navy Daddy. San Francisco, 1934.

Cop. Harlem, New York, 1936.

Mounted Cop Changing Tire for White Lady.
Harlem, New York, 1936.

Warriors. Harlem, New York, 1936.

Guns for Sale. New York, 1936.

Man in a Hurry. New Orleans, 1937.

Death Stalks Fillmore. 1934.

By the Railroad Track. 1939.

Strange Visitors. 1934.

Chinese Playground. San Francisco, 1938.

The Hand of Authority. 1934.

Traffic Patrol Boys at an Outing. San Francisco, 1935.

May Day. Golden Gate Park, San Francisco, 1935.

Lunch Hour. San Francisco, 1934.

The Depression

Lunchtime at ERA (Emergency Relief Administration) Camp. California, 1934.

Black and White Bread Line. New Orleans, 1937.

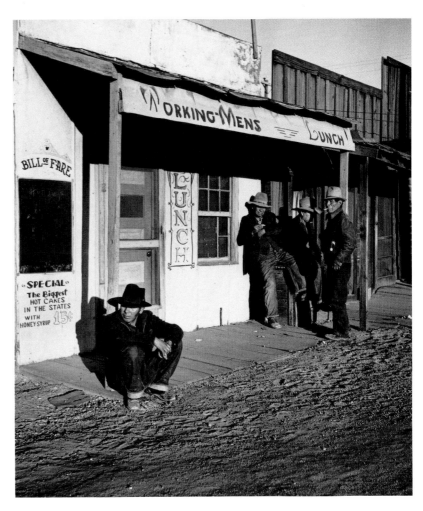

Shoshoni Indians. Wyoming, 1936.

Mobile, Alabama. 1937.

Waiting. Mobile, Alabama, 1937.

Dream of Uprising. 1935.

Men Out of Work Discuss Politics. San Francisco, 1935.

Selling Apples: No. 1 Broadway. New York, 1936.

Pickets, Maritime Strike. New York, 1936.

CWA (Civil Works Administration) Project Workers Waiting to Join the Funeral Parade for Killed Workers.
General Strike, San Francisco, 1934.

*Chow Time for Occupying National
Guard.* General Strike,
San Francisco, 1934.

*National Guard on Truck Patrolling
Waterfront.* General Strike,
San Francisco, 1934.

Produce Area Occupied by National Guard. General Strike, San Francisco, 1934.

National Guard Tanks Occupying San Francisco Waterfront. General Strike, San Francisco, 1934.

The Human Spectacle

Avant-Guard. Waterfront, San Francisco, 1939.

Before Pearl Harbor (ROTC at Mission High School). San Francisco, 1938.

Omen. 1934.

Artillery on Market Street. San Francisco, 1934.

Leap Year Parade. Berkeley, 1936.

Tee-Peeing the Vieux Carré. Mardi Gras, New Orleans, 1937.

Street Musicians. New Orleans, 1937.

Boy with Moustache and Leaves Woman. New Orleans, 1937.

White into Black. Mardi Gras, New Orleans, 1937.

The Game. New Orleans, 1937.

Jitterbug. New Orleans, 1937.

Voyeur Alarmed. California, 1939.

Majorettes in Parade. California, 1939.

Majorette. San Francisco, 1939.

Bare Back. San Francisco, 1939.

Blowing Reveille, Presidio. San Francisco, 1934.

Indian High School Band. Arizona, 1937.

"The High Hatters with Count Basie." San Francisco, 1939.

Portrait of Count Basie. San Francisco, 1939.

Aerialists. San Francisco, 1938.

The Swimmer. San Francisco, 1934.

Toward the Pool. San Francisco, 1934.

Out of the Pool. San Francisco, 1934.

Class (Olympic High Diving Champion, Marjorie Gestring). San Francisco, 1936.

Czechoslovakian Gymnasts. San Francisco, 1939.

Coed Beauty Contest. Berkeley, 1939.

The Fleet is In. San Francisco, 1934.

"Day Dreams." 1939.

"Alice from Dallas." San Francisco, 1939.

Texas Women. Texas, 1937.

Polo Players. Riviera Country Club, Pacific Palisades, California, 1935.

Stanford Coed Archery Class. Palo Alto, California, 1934.

Archery Class, Spelman College, First College for Black Women. Atlanta, 1937.

The Lesson. Central Park, New York, 1936.

Royal Couple. 1939.

Spelman College Students. Atlanta, 1937.

Japanese Girl and Geisha Friend. San Francisco, 1939.

Shrug of the Shoulder. 1935.

Two Women in Love. 1937.

Turning to Look. 1935.

Face Behind Curtain. 1937.

Web of Light. 1934.

Face Behind Veil. 1939.